Echo Booming
Monologues
100 Monologues for Teens

11/10 — 6

Mary Depner

D1293564

Jelliroll, Inc
www.Jelliroll.com

Echo Booming Monologues
100 Monologues for Teens
Copyright © Mary Depner 2007

A Jelliroll Book
Jelliroll, Inc
Fort Lauderdale, Florida
www.jelliroll.com

ISBN 978-1-60402-529-3

Echo Booming

Monologues

100 Monologues for Teens

Mary Depner

Jelliroll, Inc
www.Jelliroll.com

This book is dedicated to the teachers and students at Stranahan High School, Broward Community College, and Florida Atlantic University.

Foreword

In writing these monologues, I came to realize that some things in life never change; the way we value the people in our lives and in the world seems to me the most important element in any generation. You can change the surroundings, change the environment, change the technology, but it's fairly certain that what lies in the human heart is steadfast over time. It is our capacity to love, to care, to hurt, to envy, to fear, and to dream, that ties us together across the generations. I hope that something in these monologues speaks to your heart.

With love,
Mary

Layout, Cover and Text Design by Stefan Depner

Table of Contents

Table of Contents

Table of Contents

Table of Contents

ECHO BOOMING

The Prom

(Dramatic) Amber

Mom, think about it, I'm fifteen years old. Ya know what?
When you were fifteen, you were pregnant with Tommy.
Now Tommy's in college and I'm fifteen and you won't let me
go to the senior prom. I am not going to make the same mistake
that you made. I mean, things were different for you. And I'm
not calling Tommy a mistake. It's just that, I'm not like that. I
won't do anything foolish. I promise. Please, please. You have
to trust me. You have to let go of your fears. It isn't fair to
punish me for the things that you regret. I know you love me,
but sometimes, I don't feel like you believe in me. This is your
chance. This is my chance to show you how responsible I can
be. Please mom. You have to let me go.

The Break Up

(Dramatic) Morgan

Lucas don't. Don't touch me! You said you want to break up and I said "fine." So what else is there to talk about? You want to be friends? Friends? Friends, Lucas, don't lie to each other. That's right, lie Lucas. You lied to me. Last night, when you didn't show up for my dance recital you told me your car wouldn't start. I happen to know that's a lie. I happen to know that you were out with Theresa. How do I know? She called me to tell me. Guys! You are so naïve. You don't think she was dying to get on the phone and break my heart? Well, you handed her that opportunity on a silver platter and I came here today to break up with you. You said it first, but that doesn't mean it's not what I want. You'll be very happy with Theresa. You deserve each other.

Cheating

(Dramatic) Lyle

Mr. McPherson, please don't tell the coach you caught me cheating. I mean, I know that's what you're supposed to do and all, but I mean, my whole life, you see... (sighs) My whole life just really sucks right now, if you'll excuse my French. I mean, I don't know what I'm doing these days. My parents are getting a divorce, my sister ran away from home. I feel like I'm living in a soap opera. If coach takes me off the team, I'll just quit school. That's the only thing that makes me get up in the mornings. I know, I know, you're right I should have thought about that before I cheated. Aw, forget about it. Tell whoever you want! You don't care what happens to me. Nobody does. See ya around, dude. I'm outta here.

Love?

(Dramatic) Maria

Love? You want to know what love is? That's funny. That's real funny. Well, you go out there and find out what love is Billy. Don't let me stop you. You're real attracted to me, but you don't love me? Well, I have a news flash for you. I've been with you for two years. Two years Billy. And I loved you. I really did. And I was always there for you. Wasn't I? That's what love is Billy. I loved you so much. In fact, I loved you so much that I don't ever, ever want to see you again. Do you hear me? Get out of my house. Get out of my life. From now on, as far as I'm concerned, you don't exist.

Persuasion

(Serio-Comic) Slim

Give it to me man! I said, "Hand it OVER." Aw man, why ya gotta be like this? So stubborn? Awright. You think I'm gonna fight you for it, but I ain't gonna do nothin. I'm just gonna wait. I'm gonna wait right here till your mama gets back and when she hears what you got of mine, she's gonna kill you herself. I don't need to lift a finger. Do I now? (laughs) Yeah, that's right. You give me what's mine and when your mama comes home she won't beat your little tail. (laughs some more) Dang, brother, that was too easy. I'm pretty slick, ain't I now? Dawg. I should be in politics. Run for president or something one day. I got the power of persuasion, now don't I? Yes sir, I'm gonna run for president and I'm gonna make your mama the VP. (laughs as he exits)

A Favor

(Dramatic) Sarah

Wait! Don't go yet. There's something I need to ask you. Uh huh. Yeah, I didn't really ask you to meet me here just to give you those notes. I ...I need to ask you if you think there's a chance that I could sleep over tonight. Really? Thank you. Are you sure your parents won't mind? I brought all my stuff; it's in my locker. Well, my dad was acting all crazy this morning and I decided before I left the house that I'm not going home tonight. He's just...He scares me, you know. I mean, he was doing a lot better for a while, but...not anymore. Things are bad again. Real bad. So, I'm going to stay over tonight and try to get in touch with my grandma. If she finds out he's acting crazy again, she'll come get me right away. She's always telling me I can come live with her anytime I want to.

Thanks...I Think

(Comic) Murphy

Wow, thanks! This is great. Yeah, I love it. It's a ring. And it looks like Sterling Silver. That's perfect. Thanks Aunt Mary. Thanks Uncle Steve. Wow, that's cool. It fits me too. You know, I'm just wondering, is this a guy's ring? It kind of looks a little like a girl's ring, don't you think? Yeah, it fits, but some girls have big hands. Here, take a look. No, I like it, I do. I just want to make sure it's for a guy. I don't know anything about it really. It just looks kind of...feminine. Oh, okay, if you say so then. Yeah, that's cool. I'll wear it. No, no, don't take it back, I'll wear it. It's great. Thank you. Are you sure though? I mean, they did tell you at the store that this is for a guy? Oh. Okay. Cool. Thanks!

The Jerk

(Dramatic) Lisa

I just wanted to say that I'm sorry. For being such a jerk this past couple of weeks. Yes, I was. I was a big jerk and I know it. No, I wasn't mad at you. I was upset and I think I just took it out on everybody. Well, do you remember last summer when I told you that I wanted to find my birth mother? Well, I told my parents and they agreed to help me. No, we found her. Yeah, a couple of weeks ago, actually. My parents hired a private investigator and he found her. But, as it turns out she doesn't want to see me or know anything about me. No reason. No message for me. Just nothing. So, that's what I've been upset about. But, I think that I can accept it now. It really hurts, but I'll live.

Divorce

(Dramatic) Jen

Divorce? You're upset because your parents are getting a divorce? You know that my mom has been divorced three times, right? Yeah, three times. My mom and dad's divorce wasn't even the hardest one for me. Well, I was only two of course. So, I guess that's why. Yeah, I can understand that it's harder for you. Geez. That's too bad. I'm really sorry Dale. Is it for sure? I mean, there's no chance they'll change their minds or anything, is there? Yeah, that's pretty for sure. Is your mom really upset? And your dad? Well, if they're both upset, why are they doing it? I don't get it. That doesn't make sense. Well, hey, if you need to talk, you know I'm here for you.

Out of Sight

(Dramatic) TJ

Dude, did I tell you about my mom? She left last week. Yeah, man. She split. She got sick of my old man, I guess. Can you blame her?. No, she didn't say goodbye. I came home from work and she was out of there man. No, man. Yeah, it kind of sucks, but that's cool. No note, no nothin. Yeah, dude, I'm sure. Dude, I looked all over the place. You think I didn't look all over the place? She's my mother, man. It's cool. She didn't want my old man to catch on and all that. No, no phone call or nothin. Yeah, well, not every mother is like your mother, dude. But, she'll be back, ya know. Or, maybe she'll come to my job or somethin and let me know where she is. I want to know where she is, you know. I want to know she's alright and everything.

Campaign Promises

(Comic) Boyd

Good afternoon ladies and gentlemen. I am here today to ask you to vote for me for Student Council President. Most of you know that I am an avid protestor of the use of technologically advanced devices in the classroom. I have proposed to Principal Myers that we ban the use of cellular phones, DVD players, and any sort of device that lets you plug into music wherever you are. Yes, I know this is an unpopular opinion, but my friends, I have had it up to here. Last week, I was presenting an oral report in Mrs. Ark's class and when I finished I noticed she had a plug in her ear. She was listening to some 70's music or something and didn't hear a word that I said. In Drama class, Mr. L was pretending to watch us rehearse the Spring Play, but he was watching *Spiderman* on his laptop. This has got to stop and when I am the President, I promise you, it will.

Broken Promises

(Dramatic) Steven

Dad, I need the car, remember? Tonight. Remember? Yeah, I told you about it last week. Yeah, I did. You were watching boxing or something on TV. Dad, please, don't do this to me. I have a date. Yeah, I have a date with a girl from school. Theresa Levine. Yeah, she's pretty. Dad, please, you're not serious are you? You remember right? Why do you need the car tonight? I'm not trying to be disrespectful. I'm just trying to get things straight. I can't call her up now and cancel. She'll never go out with me again. Dad, I'm not going to ask her to drive. How can you do this to me? I'm not trying to be disrespectful! No, sir, I'm sorry. Yes, sir, I hear you. Okay. Uh, huh. Yes, sir. I'll give her a call. No, sir, I don't have an attitude. Yes sir, I do understand it's your car. Okay, I'll give her a call.

Airhead Activist

(Comic) Kristy

(writing at her desk) Why I Deserve a Green Girl Scholarship by Kristy Kooger.
Last summer I started a project called "Save the Ice." I wouldn't let anyone in my house use ice for drinks or anything frivolous. When I ate dinner out I always said "hold the ice, please." By the end of the summer, I calculated the amount of ice I saved and I think it was enough to save one glacier. Perhaps a small glacier, but every piece of ice is important. That's my philosophy. Some people don't want to sacrifice to save our planet, but I think that you have to put saving the planet first before anything else. Even before going to the mall, or getting a pedicure. And that is why I deserve the Green Girl Scholarship.

War

(Dramatic) Alexis

Why do we have to have wars? It's like there are these two forces in the world, the destructive force and the force of preservation, the nurturing force. Usually, people either fall into one category or the other. I mean, you'll have this person who is in the military and they totally believe in the use of deadly force if need be. Then you'll have this other person who is a vegan and wouldn't kill a fly. But then, you get some people who are like this odd combination. Like they'll give their kidney to save another person, but then they totally want to go destroy everyone in some other country. I guess some people really only value you for the place that you live, or the color of your skin, or your religion, or your citizenship, not because you're a human being. Duh? Right?

Money

(Serio-comic) Whit

Everyone loves money. I mean, where would we be without it? When you have a bunch of money in your pocket you're free to do so many things. I mean, it's limited of course. You know, there might be some millionaire who's 105 and he can't go surf in Maui anymore, no matter how much money he has in the bank. And then, if you're lonely, you can kind of buy friends. You could call someone up, let's say, and offer them season tickets to see the LA Lakers, as long as they go with you. But how pathetic is that? The coolest thing in the world would be to have your money, your health, and your family and friends. I'd have to say that would be really awesome!

Friendship

(Serio-comic) Ricky

Friendship is something we all take for granted. How many of your friends would you say are what you call Fair Weather Friends? You know, the kind of friend who is only there for you when everything in your world is going just great. They love you when you have money, a cool car, a great girlfriend, whatever. But if things got really crappy for you, would they be there? If your car was like a piece of junk that never started and you couldn't get a date to save your life, cause every girl in school thought you were gross. I don't know if I would even hang out with myself if every girl in school thought that I was gross.

College

(Dramatic) Mike

My parents think I'm going to college, but I'm not. My dad's a dentist and my mother's a teacher so they'll just about have two heart attacks when they figure it out. But that won't be for a while, so right now I'm playing the game. I'm applying to schools. I'm talking about what I want to study, what I want to be. But it's all an act. Hey, I'm not stupid. Why spend my last year in high school being hounded by them and treated like dirt cause I'm destroying every dream they've had for me since I was born? No way, man. I'm riding this wave all the way to graduation. And then, sure, I'll tell them. After my bags are packed and I'm on my way out the door.

Responsibility

(Dramatic) Maurie

Do you have any responsibilities? You just act so childish sometimes. Well you do. I don't think your parents are doing the right thing. Well, they don't make you do anything. Not even your schoolwork. They do not. You're always going out on weeknights, partying. It looks like fun, but it's so irresponsible. In a way I'm glad that my life has been so full of responsibility. Ever since my mom got sick a few years ago I've sort of taken over the house, responsibility-wise that is. I do all of the grocery shopping. I cook dinner. I pay the bills. And then I do my schoolwork. It was really hard getting used to it.
But when I look at my life, I see that it's really made me grow up. You need some responsibilities.

Heartache

(Dramatic) Brittany

I don't want to go. I don't want to do anything. Not even eat.
I'm not hungry. Please, just go ahead without me. Please. Can't
you see, I need to be alone. Yeah, it is about Bobby. It's about
Bobby because since we broke up I feel like....
I don't care about anything anymore. And my chest hurts. I
literally have a heartache. Literally. I didn't think that was how
it felt. I've never felt like this before. Do you think he'll change
his mind? Do you think there is any possibility that he'll come
back. Please tell me there is. I'm too young to die.

Secrets

(Dramatic) Stephanie

Everyone has their secrets. Big ones and small ones. Their skeletons in the closet, you might say. I have so many things, so many secrets. Too many I think. There are things that I have never told a living soul. Things that I don't ever want to tell. There are just some things that a person should take to the grave. That's how I feel. And the worst possible thing would be to tell someone who wouldn't be trustworthy and then you might as well tell the world. There are things that I'd like to tell you. Sure, I have a few things I'd like to get off my conscience. But can I trust you? That's the question.

Skinny Dip

(Serio-comic) Kari

You told me, Austen, that you wanted to bring me down
for this picnic, by this beautiful lake just to say "three little
words." You mean to tell me that those three little words are
"Let's Skinny Dip?" LET"S SKINNY DIP? THOSE ARE
THE THREE LITTLE WORDS? You're laughing. You think
you're funny? Well, here's a news flash for you. I don't want to
skinny dip right now. Not now, or as a matter of fact, not ever.
Not with you anyway. You are the meanest, most obnoxious,
most...WHAT? You're telling me you were just teasing? You
were not? You were. You do? You do love me? You do? Well,
how embarrassing, I believed you!! You are so crazy, you know
that?

Guys and Shopping

(Serio-comic) Christina

Guys and shopping, Those are my two favorite things to talk about. I like to talk about the guys at school with my girlfriends. We sit around and tell each other things about the guys at school that we think are cute. We make predictions as to who's gonna ask who out, or how long a couple will be together. The best prediction was one that I made when Sharon Rose and Evan Hamm got together. I predicted it wouldn't last a week and it didn't. But what was amazing was that it didn't even last a day. Can you believe that? Not even a day? I couldn't have predicted that, but I was definitely the closest.

Girls

(Serio-comic) Erik

Girls? You want me to talk about girls? Geez, do you have a few hours? Or days? Well, they're kind of complex, ya know. To say the least. Oh, come on. Everyone knows that the female sex is a mystery. I mean, throughout the ages greater men than I have tried to figure them out. And I don't think that anyone ever has. Take Henry the Eighth for instance. How many wives did he go through? Well, okay, I'm not a great historian, and maybe that was a different situation, but my point is that women in general are difficult to...describe or sum up, lets say, in a sentence or two. I'm only seventeen and already I could write volumes.

Death

(Serio-comic) Tammy Faye

My least favorite topic in the universe is Death. I once competed in a beauty contest and believe it or not, the question that the moderator Mr. Bixby asked me, was about death. All the other girls got these typical pageant questions like, "What do you think a role model should be like?" BLAH BLAH BLAH. But then I get up there and he looks at me and says "what do you think happens after you die?" No, I am not kidding. What do you think happens after you die? It's an interesting question I guess, but it isn't a pageant question. I thought I was having a nightmare. But I calmly said, "Well I'm going to heaven, personally, but I can't say what will happen to you Mr. Bixby."

Popularity

(Dramatic) Mandy

Am I popular? I guess so. I don't try to be though. I just do my own thing and hope that people will like me for who I am. I don't think I'm the most popular girl in the school, of course. Well, there really isn't one most popular girl. There's a group though, that I think most people would say are the most popular. No, I wouldn't say that I'm in the group. Why? I guess we just don't click. You know. I mean, there are certain people that I'm friends with, or let's say friendly with, that those girls wouldn't be caught dead with. I'm just not ever going to do that, you know. Exclude people from my life because I'm afraid of the fallout. That's what those girls do. They're very careful of who they're seen speaking to. To me...that's just wrong.

My Horoscope

(Comic) Paris

First, let me tell you that I read my horoscope everyday and it is always right on the money. Yep, I find that it's pretty accurate. The reason I'm telling you this is that my horoscope this morning said that a stranger would come into my life and that I would have to reveal something unexpected. Now, I get to school and here you are doing this interview and you select me from a crowd of kids in the cafeteria to talk to. You probably noticed that I didn't act surprised? Well, that's why. The really weird thing is that the last part of the horoscope said that the stranger would be "ready to depart this world for a better place and that the secret I revealed would be taken to their grave." Hey, wait a minute, where are you going? You didn't ask me anything yet!

The Environment

(Dramatic) Brendan

Why do you adults make all the decisions about the environment? I'm going to be eighteen next year, so finally I'll have a voice...but these last few years have been...shall we say, extremely frustrating. That's why I'm here today to speak out. You have been doing a really lousy job. And, you won't be the ones that suffer the consequences. Your children will, if you have any. Their children will. And maybe, if the planet is still here, their children will. But, you keep talking about what will happen in fifty years or seventy years and I don't think it worries some of you too much. Why? Because, no offense, but some of you don't plan to be here. If you'd let teenagers vote you might have a different situation with the environment today.

Marilyn

(Dramatic) Rocky

I'm obsessed with Marilyn Monroe. It's true. I've seen all of her movies and read all of the books about her. I feel like, if I had been there, if I had been born in that day and age and we had met, I could have been there for her, you know. It's weird. I'll be the first to admit that. It's just like, it's part of my wiring, you know. I started to feel this way when I was twelve actually. I just started becoming obsessed. It's not like we don't have hundreds of beautiful women in the present. It's just that I can't help feeling like my soul mate is in the past. I know there's nothing I can do about it. Maybe one day I'll meet a woman who can change all that. But I doubt it.

Rewind

(Dramatic) Hope

Did you ever wish that you could just rewind the day and start over again? I do. I wish I could rewind to last night when you told me you loved me. Before I said anything about your mother. I would never say it again. If I could take it back I would, believe me. (sighs) I know that saying I'm sorry isn't good enough, but can you find it in your heart to forgive me? To forget what I said? If you really meant what you said last night, that you love me, you would. You would forgive me and let me try again. If you don't forgive me, you never loved me. And that kind of makes the last year a complete lie, doesn't it? Do you want that? Do you want to erase every good thing we had together?

Solitude

(Dramatic) Sally

Isn't it beautiful out here? I love to come here and just sit on these rocks and watch the birds, and listen to the waves crashing on the shore. I like the solitude. To get away from the crowd and think about what's real in the world. I feel sorry for people who can never get away from it all. They get caught up in all the nonsense that's going down at school and home. You really need to just step back sometimes and pause. Take a look at this world. It's a beautiful place. If you're too busy to see it, you're really missing a lot. Look at the seagulls, the sky, feel the sand in your toes. Smell this salt air. Just close your eyes and listen to the ocean. What a beautiful sound. It's talking to you. Can you hear it?

Novel Ideas

(Serio-comic) Phineas

I've been sitting here writing all night and haven't slept a wink. (looks out the window) The sun is rising and I'm almost finished with the third chapter. This is where Ricardo discovers that his wife has left him and his daughter isn't really his own. But in the next chapter he follows his wife to clown school. Yeah, to clown school. She left him because it was her dream to be a clown and he was holding her back. And, he coldly ships the daughter that isn't his off to boarding school and then suddenly he finds out that the DNA test was wrong and she was his after all. But by then it's too late. She doesn't ever want to speak to him again. So meanwhile, he goes under cover as a clown at the clown college and his wife falls in love with him all over again. But he can never take off his clown face or she'll know it's him and it will be over. (wipes his eyes a bit) It's gonna be such a tearjerker.

Sour Grapes

(Dramatic) Colleen

No, I'm happy for you, I really am! What makes you think I'm not? Just because I wanted that part all my life, doesn't mean that I'm not mature enough to handle the rejection. I can be professional about this. After all, you got the part because you're blonde. They didn't tell us that we shouldn't even bother auditioning if we were brunette, but that's okay. No, I mean, you did a good job too, but let's face it, you didn't even try. I asked you to come along to the audition to keep me company and then you end up stealing the part. You didn't steal it? That's what I'd call it Sarah, but that's fine if you don't see it that way. There will be other plays. Don't worry. I'm happy for you, really.

Goodbye

(Dramatic) Jasmine

Who are you? I feel like I don't know you anymore. Look at you. You're drunk.

Todd, you're drunk. I can't even talk to you like this. (turns away as he is vomiting) Oh, gross. Are you okay? Now do you believe me? You've had too much to drink. You always have too much to drink lately. Sweetie, I love you, but I can't do this anymore. Yeah, I know, I'm no fun. You're right it's me. I've changed. Yeah, that's brilliant. I'm an idiot who just doesn't know how to have a good time. By drinking too much and throwing up, I guess. What a blast. Well, thanks Todd. You just made it a lot easier to say goodbye. So...goodbye.

All Wet

(Serio-comic) Kelly

(knocking)

Raymond! Let me in! Raymond, please, it's raining. Can you hear me? It's starting to rain. (looks around and tries to huddle closer to the door) Hey! I'm sorry okay. I know you're mad at me, but I'm freezing and I'm getting soaked. Please!!! Please Raymond! (looks up startled) Oh my God, did you see that lightning bolt? Raymond, at least let me in so that I can call my mother. (sees the door is opening) Oh, thank you, thank you, Raymond. (takes something from him and looks at it) What's this? A raincoat? (The door slams in her face and she puts on the raincoat) Raymond, let me in!!!!

Paradise

(Dramatic) Rebecca

There are some days in the summer when the world just seems like paradise, you know?

To me the perfect day is a day at the beach with the warm sun baking the backs of my legs as I lay like a piece of lead on my towel. Toes digging into the sand, my favorite music playing on the radio. The smell of warm coconut scented sun lotion in the air. Laughter and seagulls floating across the air against a back drop of the incoming tide.

Sometimes when I'm in class, I just rest my head on my hand like this, so it looks like I'm reading and then I close my eyes and I think of my perfect day. Sometimes I imagine it so well that I feel like I'm actually there. It's like a slice of paradise in the middle of the school day.

Him or Me?

(Dramatic) Audrey

What's it gonna be mom? Him or me? You decide. Cause I'm
not living here with him anymore. He's not your husband, he's
not my stepdad, he's just some guy who lives with us. And me,
I'm your daughter. Come on, mom, it shouldn't take you this
long to decide. In fact, just because you can't choose without
a beat tells me I need to pack my bags and leave. In fact, that's
what I'm going to do. Yes, mom. I mean it. I am leaving. Your
daughter is leaving and it's because of him. I have told you
over and over again that I can not stand that man. He is making my life a living hell. But you refuse to see it. You look
the other way. And I can't stay here anymore. I know it's hard
mom. I know it's not easy for you, but you would think you
could tell him to leave, for my sake. I'm only sixteen, but I can
make it on my own. I have friends. I have Aunt Kathy. Don't
worry mom. It's just the way it has to be.

The Upside of Cavities

(Comic) Shi

I have a crush on my dentist. Which is why I'm eating caramels. Ummm. They're so gooey and sticky, they are just perfect for my plan. You see, I was just at my dentist's, Mr. Marc Rosenthal, (sighs) and I didn't have a single cavity. You might think that's a good thing, but it's not. If I had just one tiny cavity, I would have a date to go back and see Marc. So, that's why I'm chewing caramels, and eating candied apples, and chewing gum in between. If I could get just one rotten tooth, or one loose filling, I would get to spend some time in the chair, gazing up at Marc. He is so incredibly handsome, especially when he's serious. You know that serious look the dentist gets when he looks at your teeth and then at your x-rays and back at your teeth? (sighs) Yeah, there is definitely an up side to cavities.

What Part of NO?

(Serio-comic) J.J.

WHAT PART OF NO, DON'T YOU UNDERSTAND? (laughs) Just kidding mom. But seriously, I don't want to take Jennifer Fudson to her high school prom! Please don't make me do it. I don't even know the girl. Yeah, I know, she's your boss's daughter, but I've never met your boss or his lovely daughter. Why does he even want me, practically a juvenile delinquent, to take his precious little girl anywhere? Does he know how crazy dangerous I am? Does he know I'm potentially psycho? I don't care what she looks like. I don't want to see her picture. (sighs, and begrudgingly looks at it) Does Mr. Fudson know I've been accepted to Harvard?

Firgenstack

(comic) Joey

Udvong derk Firgenstack. Oh, yeah, I forgot, you don't speak Snigglish. Snigglish. You've never heard of it? Have you been away for a while? On another planet maybe? Huvendish Loudfin! Oh, sorry. That just means, Dawg! So, yeah, everybody here speaks Snigglish. Well, some people don't, but they don't speak at all. You know, the mind-geeks. The mind-geeks. Yuven, you have been away for a while. The mind-geeks don't say anything out loud. They can read each others minds and ours too. They can communicate with you and you won't even know what you said. It's pretty scary. It's like, they could ask you what you ate for lunch and your brain would answer them, but you'll never know that you just had the conversation. I'm practicing to be a mind-geek, which reminds me, I'm late for practice.

My Choice

(Dramatic) Richard

When I was eight, my dad hired a private detective to spy on my mom. She was having an affair with a guy from our church. My dad's private detective got pictures. So, when they got divorced, my dad sued for custody of my brother and me. I was only eight years old, so I didn't really know what that meant. They called me into court and the lawyer actually asked me, "Son, do you want to live with your mom or your dad?" I sat there on the stand looking around the court room. There was my mom on one side and my dad on the other. All I knew is that she had cheated on us and turned everything upside down. So, I picked my dad. I was only a kid, ya know.

Clouds

(Dramatic) Lindsay

Clouds are my obsession. I love to fly whenever I can, so that I can get a chance just to gaze down on those fluffy, miraculous, natural works of art. When you're flying above them, they look like a giant pillow in the sky. I used to think I'd like to paint, you know, be an artist. Just so I could capture that beauty, that feeling that I get when I look out at a gorgeous sky. But you know what? I don't really think it's possible to capture beauty like that. You have to experience it first hand. Don't you think?

On the Plane

(Comic) Marissa

Where are you headed to? Oh, yeah, dumb question. (laughs nervously) We're all headed to Pittsburgh aren't we? Oh my. I say stupid things when I get nervous. Well, yeah, I'm a little nervous. About flying of course. Well, not about flying, but about not flying if you know what I mean. (laughs again) I hope I'm not making you nervous. Oh good. (slight pause) What's that you're reading? Oh my gosh! That is such a great book! But I wish Sheila didn't have to die in the end.

On the Couch

(Comic) Jonathan

Well Doc, I'm glad you could take me on such short notice. I'm really having a lot of anxiety over my senior year. I mean what's going to happen after my senior year? It's like the whole year is full of all these important events. Like applying to colleges, homecoming, prom night. And then, will I be valedictorian or just salutatorian? Will I get enough tickets for my whole family to attend the graduation ceremony? The War Memorial Hall is pretty small you know. I hear that tickets are tight. (sighs) I know I'm only a freshman Doc, but I worry about these things.

Words

(Comic) Anderson

Sometimes I just can't stop thinking about words. I mean, who made them up? Who decided that a glass is called a glass and not a ...schnogle or a bagel? Why is a teacher called a teacher and not a tablecloth or an idlerounder? I guess that's why I'm fascinated by languages. If you really want to study them you can find like 20 different ways to say one thing, like banana or money. But, of course it's still more fun to make up your own language, I think. So, I'm starting my own. A glass is a hodgeworth and a teacher is a Yoopenminer. Oh, a banana? I'm still working on that one. It's either a doogle or a lodsworth.

Soul Mate

(Dramatic) Tanisha

Do you believe that everyone has a soul mate? That special someone who just completes you? Makes your life whole? I'd like to think that's true. That everyone has a soul mate out there. But, if it is true, neither one of my parents have found their soulmate yet. They sure do keep trying though. My dad, for instance, he's been married three times. And, my mom, well she's been in and out of about a million relationships. Give or take a few. (sighs) I hope that my soul mate is the first person that I fall in love with and that we get married and spend the rest of our lives together. That would sure make life a lot easier.

Message in a Bottle

(Dramatic) Christopher

I'm a little distracted today. Yesterday, I went to the beach and as I was walking along, I noticed a bottle with a message in it. Yeah, just like in the movies. Pretty cool, huh? Well, that message said, "Help, I'm being held hostage." And it was signed "M." Yeah just the letter M. Pretty weird, huh? I looked around to see if somebody had just thrown it there, but I don't think so. I think it just washed up on the shore. It could have come from as far away as Africa for all I know. I just can't stop thinking of it. Someone's asking for help and I have no idea who or where they are. I guess I'll take it to the police. Maybe they know of a missing person or something.

If You Could Be

(Serio-comic) Flip

If you could be anyone in the world other than yourself, who would you be? Nah, man, you can't be yourself. I just said, if you could be anyone in the world other than yourself who would you be? Okay, anyone who is currently alive dude. Any real person who is currently alive. Spiderman isn't real man. Okay, any living person who is not dead, who is not a fictional character, and who...what? Who would you be? My mother?! Dude. You are weird.

The Interview

(Comic) Bud

I once went through an entire interview only to find out later that the whole time there was a booger on my nose. Yeah man, right there at the end of my nose. No, he kept looking at me kind of funny and all, but he didn't say anything. No, I had no idea until I went out through the lobby after the interview. There was this big mirror and I looked in it and man, there it was. No, I didn't get the job. Dude it sucked, cause it was an awesome job. Those busboys make a ton of money on Friday nights.

The Power of Positive Thinking

(Serio-comic) Summer

You know they say that your mind is a very powerful force and I believe that it's true. You can think yourself happy or think yourself sad. Some people even believe that you can think yourself well or think yourself sick. I think that's true to an extent. Maybe it's 100 percent true, but maybe we all aren't fully aware of our potential, so all that power and force is just going to waste. I mean, they say that we don't use most of our brain anyway. Come to think of it, I know some people who never use any of their brain at all.

Do You Remember?

(Dramatic) Jen

Do you remember Cynthia Rowe? Yeah, that's right, that girl in middle school who always got straight A's and all that. Well, I read something bad this weekend in the paper. Yeah. I don't want to be the bearer of bad news, but Cynthia Rowe is dead. She was killed in a car wreck up on Berry Drive. Yeah, it was in the Sunday paper. They said there was alcohol involved. No, not her. I mean, she wasn't driving. She was with a bunch of kids from Central High coming back from their Homecoming game. The guy that was driving was drunk. I feel terrible. I used to be so jealous of her. I thought she had everything.

Weird

(Dramatic) Reggie

Do you think mom's acting weird lately? Yeah, weird. Like sleeping a lot later than usual. Going to bed really early. Basically being in bed most of the day. And she never laughs anymore. No she doesn't. You haven't noticed? Go ahead, try telling her a joke or some funny story. She used to laugh at everything. Now, she just stares. I don't know what to do. I think she's really depressed. You really haven't noticed? Pay attention for a while and you'll see what I mean. I think it's serious, Sarah.

Dancing is My Life

(Dramatic) Seren

Dancing is my life. If I couldn't dance I think I might not be able to breathe. When my eyes open in the morning it's the first thing I think of. And when I go to bed at night, it's the only thing on my mind. It's just this huge part of my life. School, friends, even my family...they are all a side dish right now. Boyfriends? Forget about it! I mean, who would understand that I dance about six hours a day after school? Who would understand that I eat, drink, and sleep plies? No high school guy that I know, that's for sure.

The Ambassador

(Serio-comic) Carmine

I'm like the diplomatic ambassador for my entire family. Anytime there's a fight or even a tiny little argument, somebody calls on me to intercede. Like yesterday, my Uncle Vinny called me on my cell phone. Unfortunately, I just happened to be in the middle of History class. So, I whisper "Hey Uncle Vinny, what's up?" Well, he says "Sorry to disturb you, but I figure this is more important than whatever class you're in right now. Your Aunt Sheila and your mother just had a huge fight and Sheila says she's never goin over there no more." At that point, my History teacher, Mrs. Farrel, strolls up to me and says, "Carmine Ramano, would you like to share with the class what you are so busy talking about on the phone?" So I say, "Oh, nothing, Mrs. Farrel. Only the Civil War."

Never Again

(Dramatic) Lorrie

I'm never dating an older guy again. Yeah, John and I broke up. My mom warned me from the start. Well, she just said, "He's too old for you." I took it as an insult at the time, but she was right. Believe me, there is a huge difference between 18 and 38. Yeah, 38. You didn't know that John was 38? That's true, you never met him. (sighs) I don't think any of my friends ever met him. What 38 year old guy wants to hang out with a bunch of kids anyway?

If at First

(Serio-comic) Zoe

If at first you don't succeed try, try again. I'd say that saying is just a little bit worn out, wouldn't you? In fact, there are a lot of sayings that are worn out. Like, don't make a mountain out of a molehill. Or, how about every dog has his day? I hate that one with a passion. Whenever I want to do something that I'm not old enough to do, my mother says, "Every dog has his day." I just want to puke. When I'm the President of the United States, I'm going to make it illegal to say any saying that is as old as your grandma's underwear!

The Burden of Proof

(Serio-comic) Allison

Do you love me? The burden of proof is on you. What is your first piece of evidence, Mr. Smith? Oh, I see, a love letter. (looks it over) Hmmm. This letter was written to me over one year ago. Ladies and gentlemen of the jury take note of the age of this yellowed and fading piece of correspondence. Anything else Mr. Smith? Any witnesses, perhaps? Your mother? Okay, I suppose she would be able to testify in your behalf...or otherwise. Is the witness present? Do you have a deposition in her absence? Hmmm. Your honor, due to her lack of presence at the trial, and without a deposition, I move that we strike the witness. Well, Mr, Smith, in light of your poor presentation in your defense, I'm afraid you have only one option left. Kiss me you fool.

Happy Mother's Day

(Dramatic) Nikki

(sitting at her mother's grave) Happy Mother's day mom. I'll bet you thought I wouldn't remember. Yeah, I know, I used to always be so busy with cheerleading and boys that I would forget. And then at the last minute I'd make you a card and try to do breakfast in bed. You always made such a fuss. You were a good mom. Did I ever tell you that? Did I ever take the time to just stop and look at you and tell you how much I appreciated you? And everything you did for me? For us? The family is falling apart without you mom. We just took it for granted that you would always be there. You wanted to always be there. You would have been if you could have. I miss you mom. Happy Mother's Day.

It's Over

(Serio-comic) Paul

Maureen, it's over. Hey, I said it's over. No, not us! What are you crazy? The silent treatment that I've been giving you for the past week. It's over and I'm sorry. When you won the State Solo contest, you just started ignoring me and everyone kept making such a big deal over you. I just felt left out. So, I just decided that you deserved the silent treatment, but I was wrong. So it's over now. Huh? What? You didn't notice? You didn't notice that I was totally not talking to you for a week? I picked you up for a date twice and never said a word the whole night. I haven't said a word to you at school. You didn't notice a thing? Hey, you know what Maureen, maybe it is over.

As Good as it Gets

(Serio-comic) Dwayne

Did you ever wonder if this is as good as it gets? I mean high school and all this crap. Geez, just look at your parents, man. In twenty years that's going to be you. Okay, maybe twenty-five or thirty. But, man, even college, it's more serious. We'll never be this free again. We'll never be this young again. Hey, it's all down hill after 21 and that's only 4 years away. I don't know man, if this is as good as it gets, and this sucks, then what do I have to look forward to? (laughs) No man, I mean it. My life sucks right now and this is as good as it's gonna get. Dawg! I hate getting old.

Use It

(Dramatic) Ronnie

Emily, I know life sucks right now. Your parents are always fighting, Michael just dumped you. Oh, sorry, that was kind of insensitive. But it's true Emily. Your life is... well, let's just say that it could be improved. But, you know what, it will. I swear it will. I know I'm only fifteen, but I'm smart enough to know that a lot of the crap you're going through right now, it's gonna change. It just seems like it never will. But, hey, you know what, look at the bright side. You're an actress. You're an artist. You have the opportunity to take all this...stuff...I mean this pain, and use it. Use it baby. If you look at it like that, all the bad stuff that happens, it's the best thing that any actor could hope for.

Insomniac

(Serio-comic) Angel

I have trouble sleeping at night. Why? Are you kidding? Have you watched the news lately? There's a war, all the crime, the environments in trouble. My list of things to worry about grows longer every day. Incurable diseases, mental illness, poverty. You see it in the paper. You see it on the street. And then my family. I worry about my family a lot. My dad just got laid off again. My grandmother can't remember a lot of things lately. I worry about her being all alone, but I worry about what will happen if she comes to live with us. And then, I turn on the news, and well...it just isn't that easy for me to blow all these things off. I wish I could forget it all and think about something else, like...what color I want my hair to be, or whether I should get a tattoo. But, instead, I worry about the big stuff. And...I don't sleep.

One-Way Street

(Serio-comic) Peter

I'm here for your advice Mr. Quintan. I'm in love with Jessica Lake. I know that as a guidance counselor you don't usually give this kind of guidance, but I'm desperate. And you're the only one I trust. So see, you've got to help me. Well, the problem is, like I told you, I'm in love with Jessica Lake, but right now she isn't, shall we say, reciprocating. No, the admiration is not mutual. Definitely not mutual and perhaps, one could say, the extreme opposite of mutual. Well, basically, she thinks I'm a pathetic nerd. Were those her words exactly? Well, no. I think it was more like "an annoying pathetic nerd." Oh please Mr. Quintan, do you think I stand a chance?

And Then There Were Two

(Serio-comic) Amy

Mom, I can't believe this! You're having a baby? Now? Wow... that's...great. I'm happy for you. Oh yeah, and happy for me too. Uh Huh, yeah, I've always wanted a sister, but well...to... you know, run around and do things with. Probably not a possibility in this case for another 16 years or so. Geez, how long have you known? Since yesterday? Are you freaking out? Is dad freaking out? So...I won't be an only child anymore. Weird. When is it due then? Next May? (counts on her fingers) Yeah, that would make sense. Wow! Right when I'll be graduating. Hmmm. I wonder if you'll be able to go to my graduation? No, I know, it's not that I'm not happy. I am. It's just a surprise that's all. A big surprise. Well, at least you won't have time to miss me when I go away to college.

One Summer Day

(Dramatic) Annie

My poem is called *One Summer Day* and it's dedicated to someone in this room. I wonder if you'll know who you are. (begins reciting)

One summer day I fell in love. With you. Did you ever realize it? Did you ever know? How much I cared? Even though, you could never be mine. I didn't think so. I was too shy, too afraid to let you know. But one summer day, I gave my heart away and now I need you to give it back to me. For someone else, I never thought I'd say this, but someone else is in my life. And even though you'll always be, the greatest love I never had, you've got to be a story now, that I can tell. But a new love has come my way. One summer day, I fell in love. And you were there that day. One summer day I lost my heart, but everything I felt just blew away. Into the wind, into the sea. I saw us together, but it would never be. So please, return my heart, and I'll be free.

If He Can See

(Dramatic) Stevie

I put his bible away today. I can't look at it anymore. Mom, you need to move on too. It's been a year. Dad would have wanted you to live after he died. He didn't want you to die too. It's like I lost Dad and then I lost you. Dad wouldn't have wanted it that way. He loved you and he loved me. So much that he would have wanted us to be happy. Maybe if we put his things away for a while and try to look at the world around us we'll find a way to be slightly happy again. I know we can never be as happy as we were before. One day we were this great family, with all this love, and the next Dad was gone and we were nothing. He would have cried if he could see. What if he can see? What if he is looking down right now and he sees us like this. Mom, he's crying for you right now if he's looking down. What can we do to make him smile?

The Chicken

(Comic) Roxanne

This little chicken, this little wooden chicken, was the first thing that Ronald Fizer ever gave me. We were at a carnival and he won it when he threw three darts and hit three balloons in a row. We had such a good time that night. And that was only three weeks ago. And then my head swelled and I thought he worshiped the ground I walked on. So, I started being a brat. I thought he thought that was cute. And I kind of thought I might want to go out with somebody else. So, one night I really acted up and he left, and now he won't speak to me. And this little chicken is all I have left. Oh please Ronald Fizer! Please Ronald Fizer! Please come back. If you don't come back I'll have a broken heart and I'll never get over it until I'm 103. And my kids and their kids will have to hear about this stupid little chicken until they want to throw up. Unless I talk about George Edmunson. Oh dear heaven, please bring Ronald Fizer back.

Car Scum

(Comic) George

Hey, where's my junk from the floor of the car? Huh? I just wanted you to do my oil change. You vacuum the car too? That's part of the deal? I had a lot of car scum? Car scum? I had a lot of cool stuff down there. For one thing I just took Elizabeth Shoemaker to the Homecoming dance and all of her long blonde hair was all over the floor mat. I think she's going bald. But I don't care, she's beautiful and you vacuumed it up. I only got to take her to the dance because her boyfriend, my cousin Albert, had to have his appendix taken out. So. I'll never get to take her out again. Unless he has to have a liver transplant or something. Geez, can you unsuck her hair out of the vacuum? Can I empty the bag and look for it or something? Dude, that was valuable car scum. I'll never get my oil changed again.

I Think He Likes Me

(Serio-comic) Deborah

I think he likes me. But I can't tell. What do you think? This morning in Algebra he gave me his cookies. Yeah his cookies. He's on the baseball team and his secret pal gave him some homemade chocolate chip cookies. Yeah, they were delicious, but that's not the point. What guy gives you his chocolate chip cookies unless he's got a crush on you? Right? (sighs) I wish I knew for sure. No! I don't want you to ask him. How lame. How first grade! Well, okay I'll stop talking about him. (pause) But what if he likes me? Should I ask him to the dance? What if he's just waiting for me to ask? I know, I know, there's only one way to find out. I'll ask him if he's allergic to chocolate. If he's not, he's crazy about me.

Open Mouth, Insert Foot

(Comic) Rhonda

Hey, there's that new guy in my Spanish class. He's so cute. Oh my gosh, he's coming over to our table. (He sits down.) Hi. So, I heard you just transferred from Richmond Heights. That's cool. You were in my Spanish class this morning, but I didn't catch your name. Raymond Taylor. Hmm. Cool. I'm Rhonda. Rhonda Payne. Hey, is that your schedule? Do we have any other classes together after lunch? Oh, great you're in my biology class. Oh brother, you are gonna die when you see our teacher. She's new, actually, and she is so weird. Our old biology teacher retired, so we got this nut who looks like she just landed from another planet. Hey, you know something funny, her name is Mrs. Taylor. Hey, maybe you're related. (laughs) What? You are related? She's you're mother? (gulp) I knew that.

If You Were My Homeboy

(Dramatic) Tate

Hey, if you were my homeboy you would do this for me. Yes you would. All I'm asking for is a little help during a test. It's not like I'm hurting anybody. I just need a few answers on a stupid History test. You act like it's the end of the world. Like you are gonna be put in jail for the rest of your life for cheating on a stupid History test. And how many times have I been there for you? How is that different? I gave you a ride to work about 15 times last month. So what if that's not cheating? It's still a pain in the butt. But I did it, didn't I? And why, because I think of you like a brother dude. And even though everybody else in the school thinks you're a nerd with your head stuck in a book, I still hang out with you. At the risk of being uncool just by association. So, now, when it really comes down to the line, are you gonna be there for me?

Can We Talk?

(Dramatic) Merris

I have something important that I need to discuss with you Mom. When can we talk? Okay, you have a conference call from home at 3:30, probably until 4:30. You need to pick up Stevie from After Care at 5:00. Then he has a dentist appointment at 5:30? And you have a dinner meeting at 7:30 with some really important clients from the UK. And when you get home? You're backed up on your reading? Oh, yeah, for that seminar class on Saturdays. I forgot. Well, maybe I'll just ride with you to pick up Stevie and we can talk while he's in the dentist. You're going straight from the dentist to your dinner meeting? What about Stevie? Don't you have to bring him home? Oh, you're going to drop him off at the Olsen's to spend the night. Wow, you're getting really good at this scheduling stuff Mom. You almost have it down to a science. Well, if you have about four seconds right now, we can get this over with. No, four seconds, really, I promise. (brief pause) Mom, I'm pregnant.

The Wish

(Dramatic) Emma

My sister Louisa and I went to visit my grandmother this summer and we got really close. Usually, during the school year we run around like crazy doing yearbook, doing drama, softball, you name it. It's, well, kind of crazy around our house most of the time and Louisa and I haven't spent much time together. But last summer was different. We went to stay with grandma and everything was different. Everything slowed down out there in the country. At first we were kind of bored, but then we spent a lot of time talking and laughing, fishing at the pond, and doing stupid things together like skimming stones across the water. One day we each took a penny and said we would make a wish and throw the penny as far as we could, so that our wish could come true. Later that night we lay there talking as we were falling asleep and I asked Louisa what she wished for. She said that she wished that we could stay this close forever and never forget how much we cared about each other. I almost cried, because I had wished exactly the same thing.

Echo Booming

(Dramatic) Derrick

They call us the Echo Boomers. Like they've lumped us together in a category. Kind of like a species, ya know. We have characteristics that set us apart from other generations, like Generation X. But supposedly our values mirror those of the World War II generation. I don't like being lumped into a category. It's so impersonal. I'm an individual. My values don't mirror anybody else's values, they just mirror what's in my head and my heart. But, I do see the behaviors and characteristics of Echo Boomers in a lot of the kids at school. I'm actually doing a study, ya know, keeping a record, making a chart and seeing if it's true. Whenever I see a kid doing or saying something predictable, according to the experts that is, I mark an instance of echo booming on the graph. And sometimes there is echo booming off the charts around here. But, a lot of times you see these sharp variations in the behavior and it gives me hope that we really aren't that definable after all. That we are the generation that thinks for ourselves and will let no one else define us. And maybe someday, that will be what society recalls.

Who's Frida Kahlo?

(Dramatic) Karina

My date? (uggh!) Don't ever set me up again with an (signs quotes in the air) artist again. That guy was a misogynistic jerk! What did he do? Well, first of all he says in a lofty voice, "I hear you are an art lover like me." Then he starts to go on and on about all of these male artists like Van Gogh and Jackson Pollack and never even asks my opinion of them or stops to let me get a word in edgewise. Then just as we were about to have dessert, he finally, finally, asks me who my favorite artist is. So, I'm thinking, it's about time, and I say, of course, "Frida Kahlo." Frida Kahlo is my absolute favorite artist in the world. And you know what he says? That idiot stuffs his face with a huge chunk of cheesecake and says, with his mouth full, "Who's Frida Kahlo?" "WHO'S FRIDA KAHLO?" I shouted. "Only the greatest artist, in my opinion, that ever lived!" Well, everyone in the restaurant was staring and he didn't say a word. And what a relief that was!

Superstition

(Serio-comic) Donny

A really bad thing happened this morning. I don't know if I can even tell you about it. I'm really upset. Well, okay, listen, you have to swear not to tell anybody. You swear on your mother's life? Okay. Well, in my family you know we are really superstitious right? Well, one of the biggest things my family always says is that you can't tell a bad dream until you've had breakfast in the morning, or your dream will come true. No, it doesn't work for good dreams, just the bad ones. But, anyway just listen man. So, this morning I get up to get ready for school and my mom is making pancakes. Blueberry. So, I go to the table and sit there waiting. But this bad dream I had last night was just on my mind. I don't know, it scared me man, so I sat there staring. And my little brother says, "What are you thinking about?" And I say, "I had this dream last night that I got married to Theresa Ramano." And my mother, who had the plate of pancakes in her hand, just dropped them right there. "Oh my God," she says, "did you eat anything, a piece of toast, a crumb?" "No," I said, "NO," and I started crying, cause I realized what just happened. Now, no matter what I do, I'm destined to marry Theresa Ramano. My life is over and I'm only fifteen.

Your Sister

(Serio-comic) Perry

Hey, where's your sister today? No reason, it's just that she's usually hanging around when I come over. You know, annoying you and stuff. Just wondered, that's all. She's at rehearsal for the school play? Cool. I didn't know she could act. I mean, I know she's really smart and all that, but I didn't know she was talented too. Dude, I'm not talking about your sister. I mean, I am, but I mean, I was just surprised that's all. No, I don't like her man. She's your sister. How weird would that be. Besides, she has a boyfriend anyway, doesn't she? Dude, I'm just making conversation that's all. What? I can't talk about a person, without you thinking I'm in love with her or something? Your whacked. She's only a freshman. Why would I be interested in a little freshman girl anyway. And she's got a boyfriend, right? So, what would be the point. I'm just asking dude? She does, right?

If You Were a Car

(Serio-comic) Tony

If you were a car, what would you be? Seriously. I want to know what you think you would be. I have an idea, I mean, I know what kind of car you are, but I want to know what you think you are. Me? I'm a corvette. I'm sleek and fast. I command attention. People notice me when I walk by. That's just how it is. I'm not bragging, just being honest. So, what kind of car are you? Okay, I'll tell you what I think you are first. You are definitely a Prius. You're such a team player. You always try to do what's right for the rest of the world, you know. I noticed that about you. And you're always moving forward, you know, thinking about the future. Yeah, you are definitely a Prius. So, what do you think you are? You're not a car? Oh! You're a Harley?! (laughs) Okay, Maybe I don't really know you yet.

I Want to Be a Bounty Hunter

(Serio-comic) Tim

Mom, I told you, I don't want to go to college. I don't want to be an accountant like dad.

I WANT TO BE A BOUNTY HUNTER!

A bounty hunter doesn't need to go to college. Right? I just need to be able to apprehend FTAs. FTAs mom! FTA stands for Failure to Appear. I want to go out there and apprehend fugitives from justice. I want to use my intuition, my sense of adventure and my sense of duty to go out there and bring people in who haven't kept their word. People who have missed their court dates. It's the perfect job for me. It will keep me from being sedentary. You know, sitting behind a desk. My self-defense training will definitely pay off, too. Oh please, mom, don't give me a hard time about this. I don't want to be anything else. I've made up my mind. Criminology? Is that a degree? I didn't even realize that. Hmmm. So, maybe we could compromise?

I'm Going Away

(Dramatic) Rorrie

Mom, Dad, I'm going away to college and you can't stop me.
I've been accepted to a really good school in Pennsylvania and
I'm going. (sighs) I know that neither of you went to college
and I admire you for that, I really do. I mean, I admire the fact
that you've accomplished so much without the advantage of a
college education. Look around, you have a beautiful home and
you've raised three really great kids. Well, at least I think we're
great. And, I know you want to me to stay right here and go to
school nearby, but I can't. Alaska is a really great place and it
will always be my home, but I want to go out in the world and
be on my own for a while. It's something that I just have to
do. If you could support me, it would make it so much easier.
Please think about it. You guys mean everything to me.

High School Burn Out

(Serio-comic) Eva

What I do I want to do when I get out school? I don't know, sleep late? I haven't really thought about it too much. Well, I have started to think about it, but I really don't have a clue what I want to do, so...I usually don't think about it for very long. I'm not very achievement oriented. That's what my dad says. I think I'm just tired that's all. Since I was born I've been in some kind of school or day care or whatever. Everyday of the week after school it's always been some other kind of school. Karate, clarinet, guitar. I've never been exceptionally good at any of it and I'm tired of having to be somewhere all the time. Sometimes, I just feel like being nowhere. You know, being wherever my little brain takes me. Is that so wrong? You know what, when school is over, I'm ready for a long vacation.

Recurring Nightmare

(Dramatic) Denise

(tossing and turning, wakes up with a start) No! Don't! (Realizes it was just a dream) Oh. It was just a dream. It was just a dream. Oh, sorry Lisa, I woke you up. No, just another bad dream. Yeah, the same one. That guy in the mask. Yeah, it was just about the same. Only this time I think I was going to get away. I hate that guy. And I don't know who he is. That's what terrifies me the most. I wish one night in my sleep I could just rip off the mask and know. His voice is so familiar. It's creepy. But I can't put a finger on it, ya know. Anyway, it's just a dream. I sound like I'm losing it don't I? Yeah, I probably am. This is only like the one hundredth night in a row. I don't think I can take it much longer. I'm going to have to talk to somebody. I know, I know, you've been telling me that for weeks. Hey, you should go back to sleep, I'm keeping you up. Lisa, thanks for listening. You're a great sister. Sweet dreams.

Generation Gap

(Dramatic) Isabella

You're asking me when I stopped trusting dad? Isn't it the other way around? Dad is the one who doesn't trust me! Oh, really? Well, then why did I catch him reading my journal last year? Remember? Yeah, that's right. I'm not the one, it's him. It's both of you. You're just so sure that I'm up to the same stuff that you guys were up to when you were my age and I'M NOT. You can trust me. You see, your generation was all about you. I know cause we've been reading about it in sociology class. You guys are a different breed. My generation is...well, we're just really cool. We're team players, we're tolerant of others and we build things up, we don't tear them down. It's true. Statistics show that we abuse alcohol and drugs less and our instances of violent crimes are down too. You should look us up on the web. We're the Echo Boomers. And we are the best thing that ever happened on this planet.

Highway to Nowhere

(Dramatic) Donna

How do you help a friend that is on a highway to nowhere? Kathy and I used to be best friends. In elementary school she and I were always over at each other's houses. Even our families got along. It was almost like we were related. Like she was a sister to me. And in middle school, we were still close. It wasn't exactly the same, cause we had different classes and it was harder to be that involved in each other's lives. But we still hung out after school a lot and in the summer we always went swimming, played tennis, and went shopping with our moms. But now, in high school, Kathy has just changed so much. I have nothing in common with her anymore. I mean, I don't want to sound like I think I'm better than her, but it's just that I've chosen a different path. I'm planning on going to college and I'm trying to make a difference in the world. She's, well, like I said, she's on a highway to nowhere and she seems to like it that way. I feel like the only thing I can do is let her go.

High School Reunion

(Serio-comic) Brooke

You should have gone with us Tisha. It was pretty cool. Everyone was totally floored by the fact that dad's a minister. It was hilarious. They all had these outrageous stories to tell about these crazy things that he did. Like when he was in ninth grade, his English teacher hated him cause he was always trying to get on her nerves. So, one day she sent him out of the room for doing something. In a few minutes all the kids started laughing, cause he'd climbed a tree and was looking in through one of these really high windows in the classroom. He was such a character. And so popular too. They just couldn't believe he's got five kids and that he's been a minister for all these years. It was funny Tisha. You should have been there.

Sharing the Love

(Serio-comic) Josh

Hey, you guys, I'm here, but don't come near me. (sneezes)
I've got a terrible cold. Or flu or something. I didn't want to
let you guys down. (sneezes again) I wanted to do my part.
I know, I know, I'm probably contagious. (starts coughing)
Do you want me to leave? You do? Hey, that's not very nice.
I just wanted to share the responsibility guys. Share the love,
ya know. I'm not a parasite, like some people we know. Okay,
okay, so you don't want me to share my germs with you. I get
it. You don't have to act like I have leprosy. It's just a cold.
Or, well, the flu. Yeah, you're right. I should go home and
(sneezes) get in bed. But, I'll make it up to you guys. The next
project, I'll do twice the work. Alright. (coughs)
Thanks. I'll go get some rest.

We Used to Be Best Friends

(Dramatic) Patty

I thought we were best friends Caren. I thought I could trust
you. Oh yeah? Then why did I hear you say what you just said?
How could I misunderstand? It was loud and clear to me. No,
you weren't joking. You didn't know I was standing behind
you. You were standing there, with those girls that you always
tell me you can't stand, and you were trashing me. I guess you
just say whatever you think somebody wants to hear. No matter
who it hurts. I mean, I've always known that you talked about
people behind their backs, but I just can't believe that you
would do it to me. I thought I was special. Why are you upset?
What do you care if we're friends anymore? From the things
you just said, I'd guess that you'd be thrilled that I can't stand
you anymore. No, we're not best friends Caren. Not anymore.

Heroes

(Dramatic) Belle

If I had to choose a hero in my life, a role model, I'd have to
say it would be a tie between my parents. My mom and dad
are the two most incredible people you would ever want to
meet. I mean, most people can probably tell that I feel that way
about my mom cause we're always together. We go shopping
together, to the movies; she's like a friend to me. But my dad?
You might never guess how great I think he is. We sort of lead
these separate lives for the most part. He's always working and
when he comes home he's really tired. Most of the time he has
all sorts of projects to do at home too. Cars to fix. Repairs to
make on the house. So, we don't spend that much time together. But all of those days he spends at work; he's doing it for
us. For me, my brother and my mom. And he never complains.
And mom? She is always there for me and my brother and my
dad. She has sacrificed so much for us. I'll probably never be
able to make them believe it, but my mom and dad...they're my
heroes.

Religion and Politics

(Dramatic) Kato

Why is it that some people say you should never talk about religion and politics? I don't get it. Those are two of the most important topics on the planet. It just totally bugs me how some people run like mad from a little controversy. But you know what really bugs me? What really bugs me is a person who thinks they are so right that they won't even listen to another side of a story. You know what I think? I think that some people are afraid, deep down inside, that they are really wrong and they don't want to hear the truth. What else could it be? That's why some people just act like an ostrich and stick their head in the sand. I say if you're on the planet, you need to get involved. You need to listen and you need to be heard. We are supposed to be civilized. It's supposed to a free country. No one's opinion should be shut out.

Apples and Oranges

(Serio-comic) Jessica

Donald, I can't tell you who's a better kisser. It's like comparing apples and oranges. You're my boyfriend. Of course I like the way you kiss. Tom is my husband in the play. We have to kiss, so it's different. We aren't kissing because we care about each other. So, like I said, it's apples and oranges. Oh boy. You won't be happy until I tell you that Tom kisses like a big wet sponge or something, right? I can't believe your acting like this. So jealous. Yes you are, you're acting ridiculous. What? What do I like better? Apples or oranges? Okay, I'll tell you. I like apples better. Which one are you? The apple or the orange? Hmmm. You'll just have to guess. But, I'll give you a hint. One of you a day will definitely keep the doctor away.

Abuela

(Dramatic) Rochelle

What made me fall in love with him? Well, I think the turning point was when we visited his family in Pennsylvania for Thanksgiving. I mean, I was totally thrilled to be going out with him from the start, but on that trip...that's when I really fell. What did it? Well, we went over to his Aunt's house for dinner and his grandmother was there. He calls her Abuela (uh-BWAY-la) because that's Spanish for grandmother. Anyway, I just remember being so amazed at how kind and loving he was to his grandmother. Just such genuine tenderness. And, sitting there watching him...I fell in love.

Don't Go

(Dramatic) Damian

If you loved me you wouldn't do this. I don't care how much
you love your country. Joining the army and leaving me
behind is NOT acceptable. It's not possible. You can't love me
and still want to leave. Please, please. Think it over. Don't go
down there tomorrow. Don't sign up just yet. (sighs) Isn't there
something else you can do to serve? I know, I know. I'm acting
like a child. But, I'm just telling you how I feel. I think you're
the most amazing person I know and I love you so much. This
is tearing me apart and you are still going to do it aren't you?
There is absolutely nothing I can say, is there? Well, I still love
you. And, I'm trying to understand that you love me too. I
know you do.
I'm just scared.

The Debate

(Dramatic) Brian

How was my day? Lousy. We lost the debate. Yep. We were horrible and it's all my fault. No, no, I didn't do a poor job. It was my wonderful debate partner, my best friend in the world, Tim Bost. Yep, he was lousy, but I should have known. That's why it's my fault. You see, Mrs. Morris made me the captain of the debate team because I'm the best in our class. And then, she gave me the honor of selecting my partner for the most important debate of the year. Mary Anderson is the second best next to me and I know everyone thought I'd pick her. But, Tim wanted it so bad. He's my friend, ya know. So, I did the most unprofessional, irresponsible thing possible and picked him. Boy, what a dork I was. Mary Anderson and I would have creamed them.

Love at First Sight

(Dramatic) Albert

Who is that girl? The one over there in the pink dress? Amelia? Amelia what? Amelia Hightower. Why haven't I seen her before? She's a Cougar? Wow! I need to transfer schools. She is the most beautiful woman I have ever seen. Can you introduce me? Oh come on, you know her name, that's all you need to know. Never mind. I'll introduce myself. I just want to watch her for a minute or two though. I like the way she laughs. The way she kind of tosses her hair. (sighs) She doesn't have a boyfriend does she? Whew! Not that that would have stopped me. No, nothing is going to stop me this time. This is the girl I've been waiting for. This is the girl of my dreams. You can laugh. I know I don't sound like myself, but this has never happened to me before. This is love at first sight.

Tomato Soup

(Serio-comic) Cole

Hi, how are you today? Can I get you something to drink while you look at the menu? Water? Okay. (starts to turn away) Oh, the soup of the day is tomato. Hey, haven't I seen you in here before? Yeah, just yesterday, you were sitting over there reading a book and it kind of looked like you were crying. Oh, I'm sorry. I didn't mean to embarrass you. It wasn't really noticeable or anything. I just noticed you because, I like your hair. Yeah, I noticed your hair and then I noticed you were crying. (sits down with her) Is everything better today? Good. I'm glad to hear it. It wasn't a guy you were crying over was it? It was? You broke up? That's great. I mean, that's terrible, but it's great for me. Can I take you to a movie after I get off work? Great. (stands up) Well, let me go get that water and...ummm (smiling) I'll be back to take your order.

First Date

(Serio-comic) Marybeth

Can I tell you about my first date? Well, it started three years ago. No, not really. But, well, it kind of did. This really cute guy in middle school asked me out. Thomas Ryerson. But, I wasn't allowed to date until I turned 16. So this year, the day after my 16th birthday I was washing my dad's car and the phone rang. My mother comes to the door and screams, "Marybeth!!! Its Thomas Ryerson." I could have died. My heart started pounding and I ran to the door. Oh my God. Thomas Ryerson. I hadn't seen him since the last day of eighth grade. So, anyway, to make a long story short, he asked me out. And you can probably figure out that I said YES! I was so excited. I just knew that this was going to be the best night of my life. And you know what? It was.

Dancing Queen

(Serio-comic) Harlie

(dancing to some music throughout the monologue)
Hey, what's up? Do I know you? Oh, you go to Saint's don't
you? Yeah, I've seen you around. Me? My name is Harlie. And
yours is? Oh. (fairly uninterested) Nice to meet you Carl. Oh
sorry. Nice to meet you Kyle. (looks around and chuckles at the
crowd) There are a lot of geeks here tonight Lyle. (talks louder
as the music gets louder) I SAID THERE ARE A LOT OF
GEEKS HERE TONIGHT! Yeah, geeks and sheep. Ya know
what I mean? They are little sheep who follow the trends and
try to keep up with the cool kids like us. Wanna see something
funny? See those girls in the corner watching us? They copy
everything that I do, like they have no mind of their own. See,
they're even trying to copy my moves. Watch this. I'll prove
it! If I do this (does a funny dance move) see, see, there you
go! They did it! I'm telling you Al, they think I'm the dancing
queen.

Mr. Saturday Night

(Serio-comic) Joe

Yo! Sweatheart! Got any plans for Saturday night? Oh, hey,
that sounds important. But I got tickets to a concert babe. Maybe you could wash your hair another night? Okay, that's cool.
We're cool. Some other time. (looks around for someone else)
Yo! Baby! You look hot! What do you say I pick you up around
6 o'clock on Saturday night? You and your boyfriend have
plans. That's wonderful. Glad to hear it. Just kidding around,
by the way. (sighs) Um, excuse me, Sweetie, you here with
anybody? You're not? Do you, umm, would you want to go to
a concert on Saturday night? With me? You would?
Alright! Now we're talkin. You know, I had my eye on you
from the minute I got in here tonight.

Love is a Four-Letter Word

(Serio-comic) Casey

Love? You talk of love? How dare you enter these chambers with your foul mouth. Love dear brother is a four-letter word and I warn you not to speaketh such dark words in my presence. So, thou art in love and thou art going to the senior prom? Hark! My heart leaps with joy for you. I, however, have been spurned. And I will not be attending the ghastly event. I will instead, stay at home and pine. But fear not, I will not waste the hours away entirely for I am deeply moved by the words of that great playwright who hath known what it is to be spurned and hath put his feather pen to ink. Yes dear brother I have a date with the Bard. And now, if you would retreat...we wish to be left alone.

Are You Okay?

(Serio-comic) P.D.

Are you okay? I mean, I noticed that you haven't been very talkative lately. Is everything...okay? At home, I mean? Oh, I see. That sucks. I'm sorry. I'm really, really sorry. You shouldn't have to put up with stuff like that. That's too heavy for somebody our age to handle all alone. Did you tell Mrs. Summers? Well, she is the guidance counselor you know. She gets paid to give guidance. Maybe it would help just to go spill for a while. Yeah, I know, it's hard. Well,...(sighs)...man, I'd really like to help you out. You know, you have my cell number, just give me a call if you ever need to talk. Or, if you ever need a place to crash. My parents are real cool with that. I'm just...I just want you to know, I'm here for you man.

First, I Am Human

(Dramatic) Cameron

I'm always reading about our generation, how linked in we are. How connected through technology. It's interesting, but most of the time all these studies overlook one thing. I mean, I am a typical example of an Echo Boomer teen. I surf the web. I do MySpace, I'm on YouTube. I have friends in India and Israel and a zillion other places around the world that I email all the time. I mean, I'm there, I get what they are saying about technology. But first and foremost, I am human. And the way I see it, even with all of the technology at our fingertips, mankind is essentially the same as we were in the days of old Willy Shakespeare. Why do you think we loved reading Romeo and Juliet so much in ninth grade? Essentially, the things that matter to us are the same that have mattered throughout the ages: love, friendship, family and the will to do good, to triumph over evil. And we still struggle against the same human frailties: jealousy, greed, ego. (sighs) I wish I could say a few gadgets have made us new and improved. But only our actions can do that.

Stage Positions

UR Up Right	**URC** Up Right of Center	**UC** Up Center	**ULC** Up Left of Center	**UL** Up Left
R Right	**RC** Right of Center	**C** Center	**LC** Left of Center	**L** Left
DR Down Right	**DRC** Down Right of Center	**DC** Down Center	**DLC** Down Left of Center	**DL** Down Left

Apron

Audience

Drama Terms

Ad lib
To make up lines in a monologue, or play, on the spur of the moment without any preparation.

Apron
The area of the stage in front of the curtain.

Backstage
Areas of the theater behind the stage.

Blackout
All of the stage lighting goes out and the stage is completely dark.

Book, the
The script. When you are "off book" that means you have memorized your lines.

Breaking the Fourth Wall
Talking directly to the audience.

Business
An actor's physical activities. Particularly those activities that reveal her character during a performance.

Cue
A pre-arranged signal that tells the actor to proceed with an action. A cue may be a word, a sound, a light, or some character's action.

Curtain Call
When the cast comes out on stage to take a bow at the end of a play.

Downstage
The area of the stage that is closest to the audience.

Entrance, an
When the actor walks on stage.

Flat
Scenery that consists of canvas stretched over a wooden frame.

Fourth Wall
The imaginary wall that separates an actor from the audience.

Hold (for Applause or Laughter)
To wait until the applause or laughter dies down to continue with the next line.

Improvisation
To make up a scene or a monologue on the spur of the moment, without any preparation.

Mime
A person who pantomimes.

Monologue
A speech acted out by one actor.

Off-stage
You are off-stage when you are in the wings or backstage.

Pace
An actor's rhythm when acting out a scene.

Pantomime
To act without speaking.

Playwright
A person who writes plays.

Prompt
Reminding an actor of her lines during a performance.

Prompt copy
A copy of a script that has been annotated to include all of the lighting and sound cues as well as the actors' movements.

Proscenium
The frame that sometimes surrounds the opening or front of a stage.

Set
All of the scenery in a play.

Stage Directions
The playwright's directions to the actor.

Strike, to
To remove the set from the stage.

Upstage
The area of the stage that is farthest from the audience.

Wings
The area of the stage that is off to the left or the right, out of the audience's line of sight.

Stagecraft

Parts of a Flat

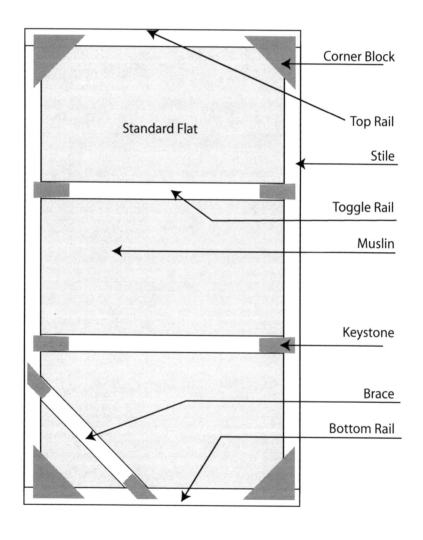

Corner Block

Top Rail

Stile

Standard Flat

Toggle Rail

Muslin

Keystone

Brace

Bottom Rail

Door Flat

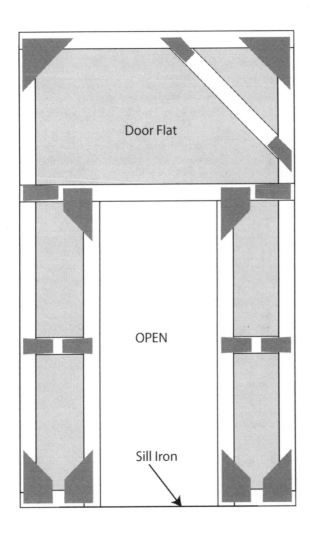

Door Flat

OPEN

Sill Iron

Window Flat

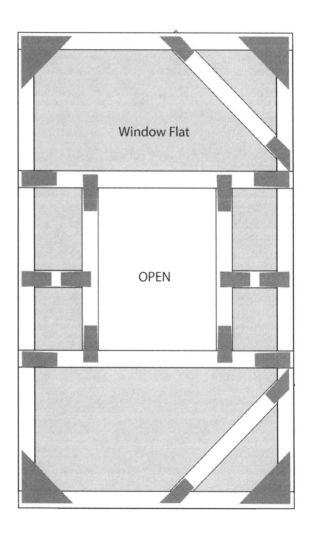

Notes

Notes

Notes

Notes

Notes

Also by Mary Depner

Acting Out on Location
Fun Acting Lessons on DVD

Visit www.Jelliroll.com for more information.

Sugared & Spiced

Sugared & Spiced

100
Monologues
for
Girls

by Mary Depner

Visit www.Jelliroll.com for more information.

About the Author

Mary Depner taught Drama in South Florida for ten years. She has performed professionally, directed countless productions, and studied Opera. She has a Bachelors degree in Acting and Directing and a Master's degree in Information Technology. Currently, she resides in South Florida.

1449946

Made in the USA